Transit

Transit

Susan Donnelly

Iris Press
Oak Ridge, Tennessee
www.irisbooks.com

The following titles are reprinted by permission
of the Editor of *POETRY*:

"Nocturnal" copyright © June 1999
by The Modern Poetry Association
"*The Sevres Road*" copyright © June 1999
by The Modern Poetry Association
"Pictures From the Floating World" copyright © February 2001
by The Modern Poetry Association

Author's photograph copyright © 2001 by Betsy Caney

Cover Painting "Stacking the time" copyright © 2001
by Kathleen Ariatti Banton
for more information visit: www.eideashop.com/banton

Book Interior and Cover Design by Robert B. Cumming, Jr.

Library of Congress Cataloging-in-Publication Data

Donnelly, Susan, 1939—
    Transit / Susan Donnelly.
        p. cm.
    ISBN 0-916078-53-1 (Pbk.: alk. paper)
    1. Title.
    PS3554.0533 T7 2001
    81 1'.54—dc2l
                                    2001003679

ACKNOWLEDGEMENTS

Acknowledgments are due to the following publications in which some of these poems first appeared:

The American Scholar: Bittersweet, Tide
The Atlantic Monthly: Harpo, The Third Prize Photograph, Samba
Beloit Poetry Journal: Thoreau's *Cape Cod*
Green Mountains Review: On Throwing Away a Bottle of Tranquilizers
Harvard Magazine: Morning Glory
The Louisburg Review: The Tile Setter
The Massachusetts Review: Chain, The Garden Statues
A New Song: Rosa Parks
Oxford American: Honeysuckle
Palanquin Press Series: The Bricklayers
Passages North: At Baldpate Hospital, Earrings, Night Stop
POETRY: Nocturnal, *The Sevres Road*, Pictures From the Floating World
Poetry Ireland Review: Time
Sojourner: Bipolar
Soundings East: Bruise
Southern Poetry Review: Lunar Eclipse
Wind: Transit
The Women's Review of Books: The Fifties, To *R.D.*
Yankee: Tea

Poems have appeared in the following anthologies: "The Tile Setter" and "The Gospel Singer Testifies" appear in *The Ring of Words*, anthology from the 1998 London Daily Telegraph/Arvon Foundation international poetry contest; "Chanson on the Red Line" in *City River of Voices*, ed. Denise Bergman (West End Press, 1992); "Soup" in *Ad Hoc Monadnock* (Monadnock Writers Group, 1995); and "Harpo" in *And What Rough Beast: Poems at the End of the Century* (Ashland Poetry Press, 1999).

"Transit" won First Prize in the 1999 Jim Wayne Miller Prize competition, sponsored by the Kentucky Writers' Coalition. "To *R.D.*" and "Harpo" have won New England Poetry Club Awards.

"Chanson on the Red Line" and "The Fifties" were recorded for the CD, *One Side of the River*, Say That! Productions 1997.

"Chain" owes acknowledgment to a photo essay by Stan Grossfeld in *The Boston Globe*.

The author thanks the Virginia Center for the Creative Arts, Yaddo and the Duxbury Women Writers & Artists House for providing her space and time to write many of these poems, as well as the remarkable community in Every Other Thursday, for its keen critical eye, loyalty and love of poetry. She is very grateful to the many close friends, flexible employers and a large and loving extended family who have accompanied the journey of writing *Transit*.

For Rachel and Patrick

and in memory of

John P. Donnelly

And a free moment appears brand new and spacious
Where I may live beyond the reach of desire.

—Patrick Kavanagh
"On Reading a Book on Common Wild Flowers"

Contents

— Transit —

— Bittersweet —

— CHAIN —

— TIDE —

— TRANSIT —

CHANSON ON THE RED LINE

The heart opens
in such unlikely places:
a subway platform, muffled in February,
the train late, no one looking
at anyone else. Then a song begins:
"Parlez moi d'amour"
like a pink ribbon unwinding
from the young black man with guitar
whose throat trembles, who holds
his head back, eyes half-closed.
We each look down
into our own longings,
familiar as the stations we daily travel,
pressed up against strangers.
Slowly we come forward
to drop our thanks into his open case.
We are shy. We don't want
to be noticed wanting so much.
            But who are *we*?
Let me tell the truth for once.
I walked here quickly
through the dark street —
a middle-aged woman carrying two bags.
I wore a black-and-white cloak
of impossibilities
that smoked like dry ice.
I am waiting here, fresh
from that swift and peopled solitude.
I can love anyone.

Morning Glory

We had a pink one
that climbed the tall window
in our first kitchen,
at the back of a railroad flat
on East Third Street.
Our bed filled the alcove
meant for a dining room
and a window was cut
from there to the kitchen,
to the morning glory,
serene in the first daylight.
That was the flat
where our bathtub
stood beside the stove
and had a wooden cover,
the bathroom behind was so small
our knees almost touched the sink.
We went to bed all the time.
I loved his coppery body,
the pink-gold hairs at the groin,
could almost feel
under my tongue
a pattern to his freckles.
Beneath the back window
our obsessed Italian landlord
raked a 20-foot-square cement yard
into a "garden," while his enemies
threw bottles from a roof.
Each morning a new blossom
opened, and near it I'd find
an old shriveled pocket.
Its lives were so short.

Once I panicked for three days,
afraid I didn't love him.
I stood in woe
at the kitchen window,
looked down at the wooden bench
the landlord had set against a wall,
so tilted and hopeless
no one would sit there.
On the third night we made love
for dessert, abandoning
the supper table,
while behind us the morning glory
drew its petals closed.
How I wanted to catch
the moment when the petals opened,
from a stickiness
drab and trembling
as the wings of a Monarch butterfly.
When he got up from the bed
and walked into the front room,
I couldn't believe I was seeing
anything so beautiful,
couldn't believe
we were here together,
sanctioned and proper,
in what I began to realize
was isolation
and the heart's wilderness.

TRANSIT

I began to take the subway
after the marriage ended. I liked
the veins of red, blue, orange, green
crisscrossing each other
on the train maps, the way
they all led to one station,
and I could get off there. I walked faster
after the marriage ended,
swinging one arm. Slept in a bed
with someone I didn't love
all funk and entanglement,
the line that connected
my stomach, his back, and all down our legs
like the sputter of light
that flies from the trolley
when it's off track. What I used to fear:
silences, downtown after 5 p.m.,
now made me happy. I lay there content
not having to worry
about love, the easy juices
within me like a dribbling faucet
that becomes a fountain, as you fall asleep,
in some Italian city. Outside his room
the street kept up its howls and shouts,
sometimes a song. Oh I was shade,
no address, derailed. But in the morning
I watched the Sunday languor
fill up with pigeons and churchgoers. I was
well-fed, no problems,
the square below rosy as skin,
nearly shadowless. A heap of rags stirring.
Going home by subway, I swayed

with the others as the train met corners,
stared in the same neutral way. But my heart
leapt up and down. City!

Saturday Morning, East Harlem

Everyone's so important. Spring explodes
like firecrackers under the wheels
of the Trailways bus. A woman hurries
from a Check Cashing store. Tulips
in cans outside the *grocería*. No patch
of earth's too small or grudging
for the troweling will that coaxes lettuces
from broken glass. Everyone's got a plan.

From a third floor, an old man watches,
as I also watch from the dim
bus window. Girl with yellow straw hat.
Three boys on asphalt, under a net.
On the storefront *iglesia*, Mary,
rouge-cheeked, showing off her son.

HONEYSUCKLE

To come across it suddenly
between one footstep and the next

at 8 a.m. on a quiet street
is to enter,
by surprise as always,

the ravishment of flesh,

but you want more
because you're mortal,
so you bury your face

in bed-tousled blossoms,
in memory, possibility,
a fragrance

that twists your heart awry,

even as a cry escapes you
from what seems your whole life.

EARRINGS

When you kneel
on the bed and start
to take off my earrings

because you want me
naked as you can get me,

I think of the day
last spring when I,
at forty-nine,
had my ears pierced
for the first time,

how the poker-faced blonde
behind the counter
took a gun and shot
the stud into the lobe.

I would heal, she told me,
in six weeks.
She smiled briefly.
It would improve me, she said,
although it hurt now.

Being with you
makes me almost forget
the way I felt then —

stunned by the loss
of what for so long
I'd pretended was love.

So you may not understand
how your deliberate
hands quiet my heart,

how I love your seriousness,

as you remove
first one hoop, then the other,
turn to put each
on the bedside table.

SOUP

When the soup burned
and I couldn't pretend
it didn't taste burned, because the house
filled with an acrid smell, my nose
quivered when I brought the spoon to my lips

and even hunger
wasn't enough, bread
torn off and crammed into my mouth
couldn't take away the taste

when I figured they were wasted, all those hours
getting down the new pot from the shelf,
soaking the lentils, measuring
cup after cup of water, losing count,
smoothing the plastic bean sack
to read, with glasses, its microscopic recipe,

and the celery wasted, the carrots, onions,
the scraped turnip with its waxy resistant hide,
the radio's Brahms piano quintet not enough,
its thunderous resolutions

as I hummed, chopped, diced, stirred,
brown burble of lentils
coming to the boil, thickening up so nicely,

steam on the kitchen window —__

when all that was spoiled
I cut my losses, set the pot
on the sill to cool. Easy come, easy go
I told myself

and saw us, ten months married
the time I made too much
pea soup from a hambone,
left the pot on the stove.
The soup grew a mold
that I shrank from touching,
so one night the two of us
wrapped the pot in an old blanket,
crept down to First Avenue
where, shoulders shaking,
we buried it in a barrel.

I'd come pretty far from those days
and alone. When the steam drew off,
and I could hold
my palm against the pot's shiny side
without flinching,

when the cooled soup
stirred up only such ghosts
as breath makes in winter,

I threw it away.

Lunar Eclipse

Tonight
you remind me
of nothing so much

as a used
powder puff
in an old compact,

pinky brownish dust
scattering
when the disc

clicks open. Tonight
I see you're a woman,
after all,

like me, and not one
who needs radiant
verses to her,

still less
to be tramped upon
by someone

inflatable. If you
could be sniffed,
there'd be musk

coming up from
tossed sheets.
If tongued

in delight, with
the whole night
starring off from you,

you'd still hold
that gathering
doubt, and cries

caught in the mouth.

Night Stop

I take the flashlight,
follow its darting path through the kitchen,
one step down into the entry,

the old blind beagle waking,
stumbling up sideways before me,

then across the porch, with its tin
washup basins still gleaming with pump water.
I'm at the bottom of a well, whose rim

is the great arched August sky,
adrift with systems. I stand
in the thick grass, head fallen back,

nearly lose my balance deciphering
a skyful of signs. Meteors

there — and there —

like the ones we'd count
lying on the beach after a campfire: silver
flashes across my eye, my breath
released as some boy's face

blocked them out. And I still can't see
Chair, Bow, or Bear,
can't remember which lessons
cover this place in summer. Maybe it doesn't matter.

My flashlight sketches
the little grey-shingled shed, its corsage
of wildgrown phlox. Beyond it — too far —

the outhouse. So I crouch in the dark,
pull up my nightgown, and the sky
when I finish, keeps circling.

THE FIFTIES

I. Car

We're driving around with someone named
Chicky, looking for a party. My mother
doesn't know I'm here. This boy Al has
his arm in a lock around me. You smell good,
he says, nosing the Sortilege. He told me
he's been in prison. All his moves
so practiced they're clumsy. Hey,
you like this? and his tongue
wiggles into my ear. I don't know him.
I don't know Chicky. We must
have covered Dorchester by now: three-deckers,
streets like tunnels. She has no idea. The hot
summer wind whips us on.

II. What We Wore

From the neck down
we were fortressed
with guy ropes and wires.

Plastic splints
pushed up our small,
worried breasts. We hooked

dress shields
over the smears
of Secret. From our waists

hung garters,
with rigging that
stroked our thighs.

Rubber girdles, crinolines,
sanitary belts
like holy medals.

III. Party

Kids spill out into the hall.
       The Platters. News flashes:
Biggy threw up. Carolyn left
with a seminarian. Hornrimmed
       Teddy C., wisecracking
as usual. A clot of my friends,
       adjusting each other's clothes.
       The steadies, Marge and Jim,
mix onion dip in the kitchen. They
never touch. Don't need to, it seems.
               There's another one
out in Milton, no one's sure where.
       A heap of coats on the bed
shifts,
       moans.

MASSACHUSETTS

I.

I was born with a birthmark
of Massachusetts, on my left thigh.
Boston Harbor, Cape Ann, a white

dot that would be Springfield
and an arm-shaped curve
ending at Provincetown. Plus a nearby

freckle or two for Nantucket, the Vineyard,
Cuttyhunk. The size
of a dime or less,

when I was an infant,
but fine-etched. By third grade,
grown to a quarter, where it stayed.

My cousin Chip
had a red mark on his forehead
that the doctor took off. Uncle Jim,

a mole with hair. But I
had Massachusetts.
I was a God-tattooed lady

and when I walked, I carried
the small map of my home state with me,
proud as a turtle.

II.

At the beach, when my skin darkened,
the birthmark darkened, too.

Just below hip bone,
at the edge of a bathing suit,
it could be noticed
without too much boldness.

A shy boy's touch
along the whole coastline
might be merely

a cartographer's interest.
I could brag about the birthmark
at parties, where I drank

one whiskey sour after another,
flourished unlit cigarettes.

In a bedroom at the Taft Hotel
the handsome Yalie found it,

cried, "What have we here?"

and I, hopelessly lustful,
displaced, aching to leave
school, to be older, to really love,

answered, "Oh, that's me. That's Massachusetts."

III.

It's quite faded now,
gone the way of the beauty mark.

With perhaps too much
ground to cover,
it has given up being a map.

But it's still one
the way lichen is,

or an ultrasound embryo,

an imprint at the beach
where somebody's sunbathed,

a suggestion on sheets.
Just an impression

on an upper thigh
of some things there once.
A memory of hands,
lips, a scatter of sand.

A place I was born to,
that has changed as I've changed,

a story disappearing
like stars at morning,
or a backwards Polaroid.

My state, that I've grown to.

THE GOSPEL SINGER TESTIFIES

When she spoke, I looked down
the way I would if she'd begun undressing
before everyone, not to entertain
but to show things about ourselves
we knew to cover. So aware that beside me
a Jewish friend listened — or didn't —
to her praise of Jesus.
I wanted to signal, "We're not all like that."
But my friend is, we are, all like that:
having something we'd get naked for
before a whole group of people.
That is, if we're lucky. So my body heard
before I did, with tears at the corners of my eyes,
as the words that had begun in song *Thank you, Jesus!*
dissolved back into song, or a finer
distillation, and the singer closed her eyes,
Thank you! bent like a bowstring,
shot forth her nakedness to save me.

— BITTERSWEET —

BITTERSWEET

When you reach for a branch
it ropes forward, drags other branches with it.
You've heard it's a nuisance vine,
bittersweet, despite its old-gold berries,
the deep coral red when the gold cracks open.

You have this life, and sore heart,
and a weather caught around you
even gold can't penetrate,
but hear your mother's voice saying:
Sue, if you want bittersweet,
I know just where to find it

and follow her path to the brambles
beyond the chain-link fence by the T stop.
Today you could see your mother's whole life
as a quest for bittersweet. So beautiful,
with its tangles, it brings tears to your eyes.

But lately your eyes tear easily,
don't they, trying hard
to see colors again. You stand here
with a long curved whip of bittersweet in your hands,
jewels at either end. And a need to decide
which end to cut, which to let spill over.

TEA

For Erika Mumford

When I see you today, we won't talk of death,
although it will be everywhere —
in your face, your slowed voice,
your hands with their silver rings.

We won't talk of love, just touch for a moment,
then a light, sideways kiss
as we each speak at the same time.

We won't talk of how I already miss you,
my heart has positioned all its guards.
Or how, because I am stupid with health,
you must hate me sometimes.

Instead we will sit at your round kitchen table,
the skinny cat sliding against our chairs.
We'll drink tea, from blue-patterned china cups
that don't match. And let the leaves fall,

in their own randomness,
into the brown pond. Let them be
birds mating. Or many children.
Or the great wave that signifies a journey.

BRUISE

Suddenly a lump
on the first knuckle
of my middle finger,
a giant bruise
turning purple at the center.
What was I thinking
ten minutes ago
when I received
the sharp blow, the crack
that made me — it must have —
wince with pain?
Why can't I remember it?
I was walking alone
in early November.
I was used
to my old heart,
the way it felt lately
as though it had bumped
— sharply — against a door,
or the edge of a table.
Did I cry out
when it happened,
raise the hurt to my lips?
Five years ago
I fell off a boat
into Penobscot Bay
and my friend pulled me up,
tried not to laugh,
dressed me in her dry clothes
as I stared at a purple lump
on the back of my hand,
afraid of blood clots,

afraid I would die.
Now she has died
— her frown, her twitching smile —
and that day rushes
like a current
past the dark islands.
I didn't even feel
the pain at the time.
Only later, when I sat
cradling the blood knot,
wondering how it got there.

To *R.D.*

Daughters become friends just as they leave.
You raise the golden spoon
and honey falls into my tea.

We loll on pillows in your jumbled room.
The cat pokes for a place
between us — unsettling books,

your charcoal pencils, a lost piece
of jigsaw. "Ah, thank you, Julian!"
Rising with grace,

you cat-step, pink-robed, in unmatched socks,
over the floor rubble
to the table, where a scene of Greece

lies half assembled. Azure and blinding white.
A landscape where the very rocks
seem to grow houses, like

myrtle springing from the ground.
Beneath stucco, pure and radiant
as a child's high forehead, the coast rounds

a bay. On a background hill,
goats and a floating column
under which you tuck the pedestal.

"Such a very helpful cat." Then
with quick-fingered instinct
you find a doorknob, beach foam, and a cart.

Why, only as they leave, do young girls bloom?
Like the staff struck overnight with blossom
which comforted Joseph, as from her home

he led another daughter. "Hold still,"
you say, returning to the bed.
"I sometimes think this portrait

never will be finished." I set down my cup,
try to assume a smile
you won't call fraudulent. Giving up,

you hand me the smudged paper.
"It's not so good." Nor so bad, I notice,
to keep your firm **R.D.** from its right corner.

But this charcoaled woman — her smile
resigned, in the tilt of her head
such loneliness. When did you catch my eye

on you this way? And through the window
behind her: suggestion
of winter trees, leavetakings, distances.

THE GARDEN STATUES

First:
Roses are full of confusions,
a terrible openness. I observe them,

try to remain unmoved. The sun
that blinds others

I stare into,
holding my sheaf of wheat.

At Father's knee, I learned
the compass, scales,

the weights
that plumb the ocean.

He impressed me
with the value of standing still,

becoming a true instrument
that takes bearings.

But Mother loved me, too.
I was a good child.

She combed my yellow hair back,
tilted my face in her hands,

   "I know you will not be proud."

Her words settled on my head
like the crown of noon

I wear as I stand here,
shutting out bee sounds,

encouraging the roses.
I feel the weight,

but I am equal to it.

Second:
I woke at midnight,
knelt among the white tumble. Outside,

warning fell all over the trees.
And in daylight

Mother would turn from him,
his bitter glance follow her.

I was ready, at his bedside,
when he showed us what dying was.

A fine actor, Father: his eye vague,
his hand fretful.

I opened my hand. He wrote on it
the death message. I fisted,

turned, went out of the room.
Hadn't I known

I was his true daughter?
But Mother saw my trembling.

I was already gathering
the cloak I wear now

as I stare down into the garden,
seeing past the flowers

to the rockhard, winterbound beds.
She prised open my hand,

gave me a fir branch
delicately fringed with green

and a stubby pine cone. I clutched them,
felt them blur the message on my palm.

Third:
Neither one thing
nor the other. Must I decide?

I am not being coy. Perhaps
evasive. I change,

I send things forth. It's true,
some buds come shooting up too early,

like a child rushing in to tell a story.
And no one listens —

so she falls back.
But there are other buds,

other stories.
If tears come easily to me,

what of it. Rain covers the sky for a bit,
then it grows new colors.

As for Father and Mother,
I gave them up long ago. Oh yes,

I always had a joke,
a tender smile, a hug.

But my thoughts were
elsewhere: testing, discarding.

I set Mother's tea table wrong on purpose.
Then beside each cup

I placed a hyacinth,
so she was forced to smile.

When I jumped up from the table,
Father grabbed at my skirt,

— but lightly. He let me go.
They always let me go.

Fourth:
You all think you know me.
Tanned, calloused,

holding, so tritely, grapes
in my strong hands. I couldn't

take leaps, look sideways.
I was neither

noble nor stern. I was practical.
My fingers knew

the workings of things. I was
"like a son." How that

curled off Father's lips! I understood.
Sons were plowhorses,

daughters, the sky-vaulters.
So I walked out into the fields.

The light withdrew
and the leaves changed. I began to whittle

with the knife Father tossed me,
hiding the little shapes in my pocket.

Mother raised her eyebrows,
then forced herself to pat my shoulder.

I showed her my wooden pear,
my capped acorn.

          "Are they real?" she asked.

I waited for her to open the acorn,
take out my heart.

"I can only do what is real,"
I whispered.

She set the little likenesses down.

On Throwing Away a Bottle of Tranquilizers

I.

Natty in your white and scarlet jackets,
reluctant magic, deadpan as Jack's beans,
tricksters, hiding each a giant-chase scene
or opening silent like a deadly locket.
I used to keep one of your number
tucked in my wallet, tissue-wrapped, "in case."
You were my touchstones, markers of each day
in that bad season. Water spills, I fumble,
breathless and white, heart knocking, mouth of sand,
buried alive up to my straining neck —
but nobody must know, none must suspect.
You my conspirator, my strong right hand!
Foot thump, broad leaf, shuddering limb —
the world so small below, my chance so slim.

II.

Trojan horses, every one of you,
teeming with men like maggots.
The footbridge down, my breath slowed,
the city hammered tight and sleeping.
Each pillow dented with oblivious head,
eyes shut neat as dolls. My heart
steadies, stops its leapfrog. Hands
come out of their clench. The fingers open:
there, on the palmways of life and love
a couple of you roll like tossed-out bottles.
The sound of running. A flare.
Ducking soldiers, in their swift crouch,
a slant of triumph on their faces.
The torching of the first house.

III.

Like a jar of conversation hearts:
Be Mine — Oh You Kid — Don't Tell
each of you held your motto:
                    Go Ahead.
Take One If You Need One. It's No Crime.
This is a Mild Dose.
                    One At a Time.
May Be Refilled. Just to Help You Through.
But Habit Forming. Caution.
                    Don't Make Too
Much of This.   Don't Drink.
                Don't Drive. The Brain —
I wonder why you seem to mind so much.
Did someone in your family take these once?

IV.

You survived three drawer cleanings,
tucked behind the single glove, sachet,
a roll of undeveloped film. Someday
I'd dispose of you. With ceremony. Meanwhile,
you were like the scapular I had once
with the relic: a tiny, disgusting scrap
of linen, torn from some saintly wimple,
that I kept thrusting back and back
behind my diaries and bras,
afraid of hellfire if I threw it away.
At last it threw itself away, I guess,
being so powerful. But you? I tossed you
with a bunch of nylons, concert programs, gum
last Sunday before supper. Ordinary.

BIPOLAR

It's time again for the shoes
with bricks in them, to hold you down.

It may even be time for a rope
attached to the couch and your ankle,

so you don't brush the ceiling.
Off with those seven league boots

in which you've been striding, significant
as mustard seed, grazing the Pleiades!

You recognize this time by not being able
to sleep for happiness. Arms behind your head,

watching the outside lighten.
Nothing serious, nothing for medication.

But bricks help, for general
steadiness, let you construct a golden

mean, a nothing-to-excess, until you're tired,
or some probe at the heart, a face turned away,

something you're scared of, brings
the whole thing down and then you can only

put one foot in front of the other.
No need for bricks.

NOCTURNAL

Letting in sadness
when you think
you've overcome it
is like returning

to the night building
at the London Zoo,
watching the slow loris
decide, over minutes,

to reach one
arm to the next branch, its
whole body following
like mud down a hill,
watching the stir

that you hope
gets slower,
takes so damn long
that it might as well
not be moving,

so you won't mind it
anymore than you do
the stars with their

year-long stories,
nor feel, anymore
than you feel
the rotations of earth.

SILENT

Meaning to take me to see Charlie Chaplin,
you'd gotten tickets to "Street of Shame."
Garbo an orchid in each flickering frame,
anguished and subtitled.
I guessed her troubles, but you didn't explain.
Afterward, you took me dancing
at the Copley Plaza. All wrong, of course.
What was I doing there at seventeen
with a sadly joking, absent middle-aged man?
A friend of yours came up and asked my name.
"Oh, this is my daughter."
I heard the real question ten years later.

RENAULT

I was there when you gave her the keys
to the new car. Your face was swollen.
Your hand shook. A bandaid above one eye.
She was cooking. You made her stop, sit down.
One of the little ones ran in, then out.
She followed him with her eyes, automatically.
You said, "No, look!"
Said it angrily. Or so it seemed
to me, wary by the sink.
She'd put on her bathrobe, too early.
Most nights now she fell into bed at eight.
"Happy Birthday, Beaut'!" — grimacing —
"and it's not just flowers!"
I'd seen the car waiting in the driveway,
shiny as licorice. Mean little staller, as it turned out.
I knew it was the last thing she wanted.
To have you well again, the beer cans trashed,
pill bottles emptied. She took the keys,
went to the door, obedient. "Thank you, Dad."
She began to cry. "Thank you."
To have quiet again. Peace. Your old true smile.

At Baldpate Hospital

When he came through the door
he looked ten years younger.
My brother and I,

the two eldest, got up shyly,
not looking at each other,
just as we hadn't talked much

on the way to the hospital.
Though he'd left in an ambulance,
naked and raving,

we were from the sunshine family
and had no words. He came toward us,
dark-browed, hesitant,

the bones of his face showing
for the first time in months.
He was wearing slippers.

He held out a hand to each of us
and we took it.
I gave him a kiss

on the edge of his cheek.
It was early spring,
I remember.

The hills around the hospital
were an uncertain green.
"Started tennis?" he asked

and I wanted to cherish
his face in my two hands
or run away

from him and my brother
into those dense trees.
He showed us the card room,

where three patients
sat playing. Told us the food
"left something to be desired."

Whenever he spoke, he looked
at us humbly. Whenever we spoke,
we looked away.

In late afternoon
he walked us to the car,
past a thicket of pussy willows.

"You like these,"
he said
and gave me a branch to take home.

PRATFALL

Over the threshold
trip, dark one,
hat pulled down,
eyes crossed

into the birthday party,
its candles flick-
ering, shy, small faces
looking up

as you, seeing them,
fake surprise.
Shadow
in shadow, open

a sunny door
to come once more
down brick
steps in April,

where early
crocuses gather
and someone holds
a home movie camera.

Clown for it,
trip, come forward
till your image
takes over the screen

and I, your heiress,
watch you leave
stagger   smile
beyond tear, or caress.

SPIKE JONES

Whistles, bells and kazoos
set out to murder a ballad
like "If I Could Be With You",
as Spike, playing bartender,

syncopates something sweet
with taps on a shot glass
at just the wrong
beat or breaks up a fight

with three different sirens on.
How my Symphony-going
Dad loves this stuff —
he doubles over, pounding his leg,

as that Cagney clone sneezes,
colossally, in someone's
face, then sounds a gong

so obnoxious the song
flies out the Ladies Entrance.

SAMBA

I think it's a samba
they're playing in the prom tent,
as I watch from the lilac bushes
at the edge of the quad.
My feet start to move
experimentally, testing
the rhythm. Samba?
Or rumba? Latin, anyway.
Not that the prom kids care.
They're just swing dancing,
pulling each other around.
Here's where I saw the comet
after my father died. A blur,
like one of those whirled-out gowns.
I wouldn't be young, that's for sure,
tense and radiant, pinning on flowers.
But am I pathetic, or mad — alone in the dark,
growing older, doing the samba?
It doesn't feel so. On his honeymoon cruise
my father was named by the bandleader
"the perfect samba type." A family joke,
but maybe he was, at that:
not tall, darkhaired, taking on weight
with age and responsibility. Just fit,
perhaps, for the samba,
its dip and lowslung
jump-slide forward
then back, that I practice now
into the scratchy lilac,
marking the soft soil.

— CHAIN —

THE TILE SETTER

John P. Donnelly 1901 — 1995

I.

When he heard that the others
were planning to tar and feather
the Protestant neighbor girl
who loved a Black and Tan soldier,
he ran, because of who he was
and would be for ninety-four years,
over the back fields to warn her.
He was the quiet brother, a camouflaged
gunrunner during the civil war,
who passed messages along the deep hedge lanes,
left notes in the crook of a tree.
Everything local, personal. He'd show
his American grandchildren the IRA medal
kept in a desk drawer, then talk of how,
outside his childhood door,
was "the biggest field in the world."

II.

For one who had learned,
in a new country, to set
tile, learned how to fit
corners, cut each smooth square
into place, round the whole
with the curved border tile; to a man
with his own thoughts doing this,
his dreams and absorbed calculations:
bank account, house, first child
a daughter who fit his arms,
for such a person, what of the crash
in the big, strange country, the Thirties'
great downslide, harsh shattering, loss
of customers, house gone, second child coming,
wife's stony eyes, all the tiles
rubbling down and the tile dust blinding?

III.

When his daughter-in-law first met him
he was coming in from his shift
at the Railway Express,
where he'd labored for twenty-five years.
He stumped off his boots
in the back hall — it was December, and snowing.
"You can come right in, John,"
his wife called, "She's a regular girl."
He came in, wearing workclothes, his face drawn,
very pale, held out his hand in welcome.
He was all bent inward in those years,
as though tons of boxes and parcels
had been lowered, one by one,
onto his shoulders at the station.
Like the medieval Celtic trials
to prove poets: that they bore
in a pit, under a testing of stones.

IV.

Then, in early old age, he finds
the falling-down little house he can fix over.
Rooms that, once cleaned, cry out
for tile, tile everywhere:
above kitchen counters, up the stairs,
a riot in the bathroom, lining the basement shower.
Once that's all set, he goes out
on early spring mornings — he's retired now —
to yard sales, brings back
small tables of every shape, just waiting
to be tile-covered. Blue, cream, brown-speckled,
dusted with gold, they fly off
as wedding presents, gifts to nieces.
There are always new patterns.
Under each table he paints
a huge shamrock, "John P. Donnelly," the date.

V.

"Maureen," his whispered protest, "I'm still not dead…"
He's off-schedule, impatient. He told his daughter
yesterday he'd not live past midnight.
Now here's the city sun, filled with haze,
coming through dull hospital curtains.
Down Cloone's main street it would pour
clear honey till ten at night…
He's let so much go:
the hard marriage, little house, apartment
full of trailing plants and Irish tea towels,
big TV for watching Notre Dame.
He's left his zinnia garden,
planted along the parking lot. That design
of colors. Left his canopy bed.

ANCESTOR

Youghal, Ireland, 1839

Resistance to them all.

I turn from the rail at the stern
where everyone's weeping. They shade their eyes
against the light from the east,

as I step away,
move toward the forward deck.
Nothing to say, nothing to keep down
but breakfast. From here on in,

no shamrocks. And only new songs.
That's how I am, God help me,
to those that leave me. Even countries.

Stone-cold as jade.

Thoreau's *Cape Cod*

Death's is the long arm
that reaches across the book. Over his tramp
through the pulling sands of Nauset,
beneath his catalogues of beach pea and spurge,
the carcass lies
tossed onto the shore.

He had seven more years. The ocean took such time
over its catch! "There is no telling
what it might not vomit up."
Cods full of nutmegs,
a bottle "stopp'd tight and half-full of red ale,"
towcloth, turnip seed,
and a lost anchor
that "sunken faith and hope of mariners."

The Cape's arm reached toward something
beyond land. A fisted curve,
with the smack of the unpredictable Atlantic
coming up against its outside.
And what the fist tried to hold
fell through in grains
as every year changed
the shape of the beaches.
What if in Provincetown dexterous ladies
"emptied their shoes at each step"?
There was nothing

constant
as his own deep pond.

Massachusetts Bay
was a maw of foundered ships,
a death's cradle of immigrants,
slung back and forth with a stark rocking,
that tore from them
their poor clogs and lockets,
threw them to purify
into pale ivory on its beaches.

It was the leaping ground
of the Howling Whale
that all the little boats hounded to shore,

to render from each
a hundred-dollar barrel of oil,

then leave them,
opened and rotting,
warning off walkers with their stink.

      "The annals of this voracious beach!
        Who could write them?"

Against the glass
of even the Highland Light
"nineteen small yellowbirds"
broke their necks one night.

Back home in Concord, he walked always to the West,
sniffed out a new trail each day.

Here with "all America behind him,"
a man could stumble for hours over the dunes
and die at last
in a charity hut,
one arm outstretched to the cold hearth.

TIME

"It's time to move forward," said Cain,
kicking aside a turnip,
"time to put the past
behind us." He frowned at his parents.
Where else would it be then? they wondered,
who'd had only scraps of it
and a desolate future.
"Yes, time," said Cain again

and walked away. Attila, too, cried "Now
let there be healing!" on a hill
above a smoking village.
He and his soldiers could still
smell roasted flesh,
pick out here and there
a lump twitching. "Time,"
— he swung one blood-smeared arm wide

over the quick and dead —
"to come together as one people…"
"In short, reconcile!" snapped Cromwell,
who measured ambition
by the tree-dwelling, feckless Celts.
Himmler fanned his face:
"Ja, it is here too scorching. Let us move on."

CHAIN

In the middle of nowhere,
in the middle of God's parched earth,
young shackled women prisoners
bury the homeless. And cry.
The Arizona sun slams down,
even their clothes are barred, it takes
eight of them at the sides and one at the end
to carry each plain coffin.
Here is a case where nowhere's
better than somewhere,
if somewhere's a cell. When they cry,
a crewcut, middle-aged clergyman,
gathers them loosely in his arms.
One of those Jesus railed against.
Or maybe any comfort's better than none,
as the smack of free air
is better, though clogged with dust.
Because the women are young,
even a baby-step, sideways, carrying a coffin,
gets their blood moving. Not quite
paupers, they weep for paupers.

To hell with the guard,
whose shadow holds a gun.
To hell with the man of God.

Rosa Parks

What you continue to do
is make me understand
that one day there may be a moment,
unannounced, for each of us. A small occasion,
nothing glamorous. When we're tired,

rather fed-up, and with a rush of blood,
decide. Something as simple

           — but what was simple then? The everyday
           was what required laws —

as a bus ride, a choice of seat. You endorse
dailiness. Take that first step. Rules

fall away on either side and you're left,
stubborn, on a somehow known path.
The bus brakes. They take you off
to jail. But within you it's open country,
wind blowing, road leading on forever.

The Chinese Child in the Library

Though her father settles her here
each morning, one finger to his lips,
when she opens her workbook,
she soon starts to click her pink sandals
over and over, like snapping gum.
It's the smallest of sounds in the Reference Room,
like those under-the-breath clapping games
little girls play facing each other
in church, or when adults are talking:
Miss Sue Miss Sue Miss Sue from Alabama.

In thirty years this child
will have written her second novel,
called *The View From That Window*.
Or linked two chromosomes, changing lives.
Or just rested one day, staring back to the big room
where her dead father left her safe
at a long table by the window,
her work laid out before her, a docile silence,
the pleasant small shadow of pen against paper,
then the click, the forbidden click, of her sandals.

DANCER LOOKING AT THE SOLE OF HER RIGHT FOOT

Degas sculpture

Unless you're a dancer
this is not easy. Try it sometime.
For a moment I do, before the display case
where she stands alone as we circle her.
I'm a tourist, so it doesn't matter
if I look like a fool. I need to get
the feel of the thing,
how an ideal body would do it
in one smooth twist. I give up,
stiffly, but note it in my journal.

She, of course, holds the motion
staring down at the foot's small pad
for a splinter, maybe,
from the practice floor. Or a crease
where a shoe's been pinching.
Whatever it is, she'll get to the bottom of it
before she unwinds, shakes herself,
starts moving again.
Her face, examining,
is the realest face she has.

THE BRICKLAYERS

The bedspread
patterns my face
with little crosshatches
as I lie here listening

to the click and rattle
of their hammers on brick,
to their whistling
as I fit and tuck

my life into my life.
Their hammers counterpoint,
as I measure the sidewalk
on my knees, in my own

string-marked plot.
They joke together
as I eavesdrop asleep,
take their sound over me

like a body,
still dusty,
sweaty and gentle,
laughter in my ear.

TUNE

Hearing you hum to yourself,
one hour into our first meeting,
as you walk off to get something to show me,
who sits, with a leftover smile and flushed cheeks,
on the couch in your living room,
hearing that ease and content
is a gift to my heart
so close, so delicate
I do nothing but note it,
the way one touches the petal of an opening tulip
because of its satin, its brevity,
and, inside, its flame.

THE MOON OVER BRASS VALLEY

from a WPA guide to Western Connecticut

The moon over Brass Valley
is nearly full tonight. Is a button,
stamped with the insignia of silence,

moves over the village that turned out
millions of pins each day, over the molten city
that was "no melting pot," over the Indian graveyards.

So many moons reflect off the heads of those pins,
dance up from the stir of waters
on Waramaug, Wanonskopomis. This one is stunted

like the hand caught in the button press. Could howl
with the five-legged dog from the witch village.
Or bloat and turn orange against the horizon

like the last pumpkin. But tonight
it's a hunchbacked peddler, scooping up
belt buckles, doorknobs, brooches

from all over the Valley,
featuring the new Dollar Watch out of Waterbury:
silverplate, sturdy, affordable

by just about anyone.

— TIDE —

HARPO

That's right. When words don't say it,
stop talking. Become beautiful and strange.
The one of sudden arrivals,
announced by a horn.

A faun, seen between trees.

Pluck your thin music, your eyes
getting rounder, face changing
like clouds. And when lies
don't work, even silent ones,

get caught silver-handed,
with everything tucked up your sleeve.

MOONDOG

He just stood there,
at the corner of 43rd Street
and Sixth Avenue,
nearly seven feet tall,
dressed as a Viking.
Everyone, it seemed,
in New York in the '60s
knew Moondog. They said
he'd been a stockbroker,
from a rich family.
They said he was blind.

I was writing a novel that year,
but didn't know how,
and falling in love,
and everything moved so fast,
but the Viking was motionless.
I know he wrote songs,
but I never heard any.
He just stared outward.
I'd wake up, write myself dizzy,
then go walking, fast,
through the streets.

One day, a stranger
stopped me: JFK had been shot!
This was in midtown. The bells
of St. Patrick's began tolling
and I joined all the others
going up the cathedral steps.
I'd seen the President
just last month — young,

glinting like silver,
in a limousine going up Madison
to the Hotel Carlyle.
He waved to all of us
and we waved back, cheering...

Or are these tears
for the broken love,
the unreadable novel?
Anyway, the years.

PICTURES FROM THE FLOATING WORLD

Ukiyo-e prints by Harunobu

Everything suggests something else,
if you know how to see it.
A hand towel filling with breeze
suggests a sail, maple leaves a season.
Together: separation and grief.
But nothing too real is explored
too deeply. Those girls, stringing
a cat's cradle, wild geese in the distance,
suggest a lute plucked in early spring,
at the edge of a river, by the young
prostitutes of Edo, in their off-hours.
The viewer would have known
the song they sing by just these hints
and walked away, humming.

The Sevres Road

Camille Corot's painting
stolen from the Louvre, May 1998

It might have always been meant
that they walked completely away,
this man on horse, woman with basket.
With their backs to us and the painter,
they are so private. But like those stories
where children step right into a picture
and, looking over their shoulders,
see the consoling frame,
these two would know the way home
like the palms of their hands, the routine
so ordinary it most encloses,
no need for thought, only motion
and the full sensation of sun
on your flesh, along the usual road.

The Third Prize Photograph

I would give this First Prize:
the couple at odds, clearly,
while someone at the end of the same bench
looks off toward the river,
a cyclist goes by on the path.
Boxes within boxes,
like an antique camera,
for of course there was also
the photographer, who chose this print
from the contact sheet,
and now there's a viewer
with her own stories.
It may be that no one
knows quite what is going on,
nor what choices
lead to the moment the lens flies open —
the woman's dismissing hand,
the man urgently leaning,
an eavesdropper stiffened,
one foot bent sideways,
the cyclist in his own world.

ORPHAN ISLAND

I want to say something about love,

but can only see the orphan boys,
their tough and sorrowful faces
in the picture at the island school.
I want to tell how, shocked awake
in middle age, I got up from my old parents
to stand at the bow of the tour boat
as the island came closer. "We're so glad
you're with us," my mother said
and her hand, touching mine,
was weighted with thick dark veins.
I scarcely heard her. For him,
for a love who didn't matter,
I left father and mother. I stumbled
from the tour group out across a field,
dizzy with that branding, my breath
smacked out of me, the way a gale
hits or a breaker smashes. I wanted
so much to believe the place was wild,
but it was just my kind of distance,
a half hour from home. Still,
any island is far enough, I suppose,
or must have seemed so to those children,
who "each had his little garden,"
their faroff city lives
jutting up across the harbor like weeds.
And how the white rabbit appeared
in my path, suddenly — one of a race
of pet rabbits gone wild.

I look back and my parents smile.

TIDE

If I don't catch it
right now, the look of the bay
at the lowest tide,
with the sun stamping on it,
the uncovered sand like clay,

if I let it go
for some more important thing,
or just look away
for a bit, mean to note it
when I've first done something else,

only my mind's eye
will be left to remember,
when the tide has turned,
how the whole bay looked
like a great shell lying there —

all blue, brown, silver
and how I needed to shape
something I could hold
and keep, maybe, from those few
moments before it all changed.

ABOUT THE AUTHOR

SUSAN DONNELLY was born and raised near Boston and lived in New York City and Orange, New Jersey for several years before returning to the Boston area in 1975. Her first book of poetry, *Eve Names the Animals*, won the inaugural Samuel French Morse Prize from Northeastern University and was published by its press in 1985. The title poem of that collection is included in *The Norton Introduction to Poetry* and *The Norton Introduction to Literature, Sixth Editions*. Donnelly has also written two chapbooks, *tenderly pressed, a Memoir in Poetry* and *The Ether Dome* (Every Other Thursday Press, 1993 and 2000).

She has published in many magazines, anthologies and textbooks, including *The Atlantic Monthly, The American Scholar, Ploughshares, Poetry, The Massachusetts Review, The Louisville Review, Oxford American, Vital Signs* (University of Wisconsin Press 1989) and *Literature: Reading Fiction, Poetry, Drama and the Essay* (McGraw Hill, 1995). Her poetry has been published in Ireland, England and France, recorded on the CD "One Side of the River" (Say That! Productions 1997), and been set to music by composer Joelle Wallach and performed at Lincoln Center. The title poem of *Transit* won the 1999 Jim Wayne Miller Prize in Poetry from the Kentucky Writers' Coalition and was published in *Wind*. Donnelly's poetry also appears online at several websites, including *Atlantic Unbound* and the *Poetry* website.

She has been a Fellow on several occasions at colonies such as The Virginia Center for the Creative Arts, Yaddo and The MacDowell Colony. She has received two Hazen Fellowships in Poetry from Mount Holyoke College and a Professional Development Grant from the Massachusetts Cultural Council. The founder of the 21-year-old writers workshop, Every Other Thursday, she lives, writes and teaches poetry in Cambridge, Massachusetts.